LEARN EMPATHY

BUILDING SKILLS FOR CARING

Daniel Keeran, MSW

College of Mental Health Counseling

Vancouver - Kona - Rome

ISBN-13: 978-1470134341

ISBN-10: 1470134349

Printed in the United States of America.

Consultation and support at *no charge* is available by email contacting the author at collegemhc@gmail.com

This book is dedicated to

my mother and father, Ruth and Melvin Keeran,

who taught in public schools for many years.

Table of Contents

Introduction: What Is Empathy?

Lesson Objectives:
1. To understand empathy.
2. To acquire an increased sense of empathy for the emotions and circumstances of others.

Note to teacher: Why teach empathy? The ability to have empathy is important as a foundation for caring and compassion between and among students and contributes to positive relationships in all areas of life. Empathy builds a sense of community and reduces the tendency to discriminate or exclude others. A student who bullies or excludes others can benefit from being aware of the emotions of a potential victim and to value those emotions.

While some students may have difficulty feeling or communicating sincere empathy more than others, all students will derive some benefit from the exercises in this lesson.

Select those exercises that correspond to the overall capacity of the age group and re-word exercise descriptions for the comprehension level of the group.

On completing the lesson, at our website please provide your brief comments on the outcome and impact on students so that others can be encouraged to use this important lesson.

Empathy Definition: To sincerely and accurately feel and reflect the specific emotion(s) of another person. Empathy also means to value others' emotions.

Class Discussion:

1. What is empathy? How are empathy and sympathy different? Empathy is not sympathy. Empathy means to *feel the emotion* of another person. Sympathy means to *agree with the thoughts* of another person.

2. Empathy means that you must set aside your own thoughts and feelings and pay attention only to the other person's thoughts and feelings. Why does this ability require inner strength?

3. How is empathy communicated? Empathy is communicated in the sincere accurate reflection of the emotions of another person, conveyed in accurate facial expressions for the emotions, accurate voice tones for the emotions, and accurate words for the emotions.

4. How are thoughts different from emotions? Emotions are not thoughts. Emotions are sensory experiences in the mind and body such as relaxed, fear, caring, anger, guilt, happy, sadness, confident, low self-worth, hopeful, despair. Thoughts are ideas about another person, thing, or situation.

5. What is sincerity and why is it important? Sincerity means to be genuine, to truly value the other person's feelings as important, and to take his or her feelings seriously. If sincerity is missing, then empathy will not be communicated.

6. Are emotions OK? Yes. Emotions are neither good nor bad. Having emotions is an important part of being human. Believing this is necessary in order to have sincere empathy for another person's feelings. What you *do* with an emotion can be healthy or unhealthy.

Exercises For Empathy Training

Exercise One: Building Your Emotion Vocabulary

Description: The teacher introduces the exercise by saying that having a vocabulary of words for different emotions, is helpful for making sentences that communicate empathy. Many feeling or emotion lists can be found on the internet.

Emotions can be separated into categories of pleasant and painful feelings. For example, pleasant emotions are: happy, excited, peaceful, relaxed, calm, hopeful.

Examples of painful emotions are: fear, anger, guilt, sad, empty, low self-worth, and despair.

An acronym can be used to help remember a list of words. For example, the acronym FAGSELD is a way to remember the painful emotions listed above.

> **More information:** Painful feelings can be divided into hard and soft emotions. Examples of hard painful feelings are anger, frustration, irritation, and annoyed, while examples of soft painful feelings are fear, sadness, guilt, emptiness, low self-worth, and despair.

Invite class members (in class or as an assignment) to make a list of emotions or feelings they have about different experiences during the day. Examples: waking up, getting dressed, smelling breakfast, getting on the bus, hearing people arguing, hearing people laughing, entering the classroom, sitting at the desk, listening to the teacher, going to recess, taking a test, having lunch, doing homework, seeing parents, playing with friends, sitting down to dinner, going to bed.

Post-Exercise Discussion:
1. What do you realize about emotions and experiences?
2. Why is it important to be aware of your emotions as you feel them in the moment?
3. How does being aware of your own emotions affect the way you understand other people and things that happen in their lives?

Assignment: Make a list of your experiences between the end of class today and the next class meeting and then write the emotions related to each experience.

Exercise Two: Distinguishing Emotions and Thoughts

Description: In this exercise, class members are asked to make three sentences beginning with "I feel" followed by a *feeling word* such as happy, sad, frustrated, or other emotion.

Examples: "I feel happy when it's time to play."
"I feel excited when I get to do math."
"I feel sad when my friends have to go home after visiting."

More information: Remember that a thought, instead of an emotion, is expressed if "I feel" is followed by the word "that" rather than a feeling word. The phrase "I feel that....," really means "I think" or "I believe."

If you begin a sentence with "I think" followed by an idea such as "I think this subject is interesting" or "I think this class is fun," you are communicating a thought instead of an emotion.

Post-Exercise Discussion:
What is the difference between a thought and a feeling? A thought is an idea. A feeling is an emotion.

Exercise Three: Making Sentences for Empathy

Description: Practice making sentences that communicate empathy using this form and words from the feeling list. Fill in the blanks, followed by checking to see if you are accurate:

"You feel_____ because _____. Is that what you feel?"

Scenario examples: Here are examples of two scenarios followed by examples of sentences that show empathy and checking for accuracy.

1. Jill has a frown on her face and says her best friend just moved away.

Empathic reflection: "Jill, you feel sad because you best friend just moved away. Is that what you feel?"

2. Dad is very quiet when he comes home from work and says he just lost his job.

Empathic reflection: "Dad, you feel worried because you lost your job. Is that what you feel?"

Practice Scenarios: After each scenario below, write a sentence that shows empathy followed by checking to see if you are accurate.

1. Your brother comes home crying and then says he was called hurtful names at school.

2. The boy at school that others just called hurtful names, is sitting quietly and looking down.

3. Your friend says he does not want to go home because he received low scores on his report card.

4. Your friend says she can't invite you over because her Mom doesn't feel well.

5. A classmate at school is sitting alone at lunch time and not eating his lunch.

Post-Exercise Discussion:
1. What questions do you have about writing a sentence that shows empathy?
2. Why is it important to check to see if you are accurate?

Exercise Four: Role Reversal

Description: In the Role Reversal exercise, empathy skills are increased when individuals are asked to imagine he or she is someone else who will be interviewed in pairs. The class is divided into pairs, and each person takes turns telling the other person basic personal information in answer to a brief set of questions. Then each person imagines he or she is the other person and speaks to the class in the first person as if he or she is the other person. Mary interviews Rosie and then presents herself as if she is Rosie by saying, "My name is Rosie. I am 12 years old," etc. Then Rosie does the same by saying, "My name is Mary. I am 12 years old," etc.

Accuracy is important for building empathy skills in this exercise.

The following is a list of basic questions for collecting basic personal information:

1. What is your name?
2. What is your age?
3. What is your favorite color?
4. How many brothers and sisters do you have?
5. Where did you go on vacation?
6. What do you like to do most?

Demonstrate to the class:

"Now I need a volunteer to show you what role reversal looks like. Who would like to volunteer?" The teacher asks the above questions to the volunteer as you sit together in front of the class. Then the teacher presents herself as the student speaking in the first person and relating the information collected in the interview using the questions above.

Then the teacher says, "What questions do you have about what you will be doing?"

Instructions to the class:

"Now I want you divide into pairs and interview each other using these questions (written on the board or printed handout). Remember what the other person says, and then you will present yourself as if you are the other person starting with the name and so on. You will have to listen very carefully and remember what the other person said. What questions do you have about what I am asking you to do?"

Post-Exercise discussion:
1. What was it like hearing your partner speak as if he or she was you? Was he or she accurate?
2. What was it like being your partner? What did you feel or think when you were being someone different than yourself?

Exercise Five: Doubling

Description: In the Doubling exercise, similar to the Role Reversal exercise, the students build empathy skills by becoming a double or alter ego for another person. This is done by inviting students to walk around the room in pairs (or to sit in chairs in parallel position) while one speaks as the other doubles.

The speaker talks about a happy memory or expected future event. As the speaker is talking, the Double also talks in the first person as if he or she is also the speaker and reads between the lines by inserting feeling words.

Example:

Speaker: "I am going to visit my grandparents next week."

Double: "And I feel happy."

Speaker: "My grandma makes the best cookies."

Double: "I am excited to eat the cookies."

The speaker can let the Double know if she or he is accurate or not by saying what the accurate feeling is.

Demonstrate to the class:

"Now I need a volunteer to show you what Doubling looks like. Come here and sit with me (chairs in parallel position facing the class). Talk about a happy memory or something you look forward to in the future."

As the volunteer talks, the teacher speaks in the first person as if she or he is the student and fills in feelings or emotions not spoken by the volunteer.

After a brief while, the teacher turns to the class and says, "What questions do you have about what I am asking you to do?"

Instructions for the class exercise:

Divide the class into pairs, and as they are engaged in the exercise, let them know when to switch roles with one as the speaker and the other as the Double.

Post-Exercise Discussion:
After each person has had an opportunity to experience both roles (speaker and Double):
1. What was it like being the speaker and hearing the Double speaking as yourself?
2. What was it like being the Double? What was the hardest part?
3. How did the exercise of Doubling help you understand the other person?

Exercise Six: Listening with Empathy

Description: Practice listening to another person talk about something that is personally important, and make sentences for empathy that reflect his or her emotions. Remember that empathy means to set aside your own thoughts and feelings and to pay attention to what the other person thinks and feels.

Demonstrate to the class:

"Now I need a volunteer so that I can show the class what a sentence for empathy sounds like. Think of something you can say about what is important to you or something that happened or you hope will happen in the future. Who would like to volunteer?"

After a brief demonstration, thank the volunteer and ask the class, "What questions do you have about what you will be doing?"

Instructions for the class exercise:

"Now we will practice making sentences for empathy. I want you divide into pairs. One of you will speak for a little while and the other will listen. The speaker can talk about something that happened last night or today or something in the future. The listener will make a sentence for empathy and check to see if it is accurate. Then I will tell you when to switch, with the speaker becoming the listener, and the listener becoming the speaker. Remember that empathy means to set aside your own thoughts and feelings and to pay attention to what the other person thinks and feels."

After giving instructions, ask the class, "What questions do you have about what you will be doing?"

Post-Exercise Discussion:
1. What was it like being the speaker and hearing the listener make sentences for empathy (reflections)?
2. What was it like being the listener? What was the hardest part about it?

More information: In making an empathic reflection, an overstatement of the other person's thoughts and feelings can give added support when the reflection is accurate and sincere. This involves seeing implications of what the speaker says and including these implications in the sincere reflection while being careful to check for accuracy. If the empathic reflection is an understatement and leaves out accurate basic information given by the speaker, the speaker will feel a lack of empathy and support.

Additional exercises can be created to assist class members to recognize and reflect empathy for different specific emotions such as fear, anger, guilt, sadness, celebration, humiliation, and others. See an exercise for empathizing with anger below.

Exercise Seven: Becoming Another Character

Description: In this exercise members are asked to break into groups of three to do the following:

1. Write the dialogue for and then enact a scenario for three people: a victim, a bully, and an observer.
2. Each group enacts the scenario three times. Each time the scenario is enacted, each person rotates to take on the role of a different character.
3. After all scenarios are enacted with each person rotating to each role, each person then discusses what it was like to take on the role of each character, what emotions were felt, and what thoughts came up in each role.

Post-Exercise Discussion:
1. What emotions did you feel as the bully?
2. What emotions did you feel as the victim?
3. What emotions did you feel as the observer?
4. What decisions have you made after doing this exercise?

Exercise Eight: Understanding the Story

Description: This exercise is about understanding the story of another person. *"An enemy is someone whose story you have not heard."*

1. Ask members of the class to think (and write) about someone they are afraid of or someone with whom they do not want to be friends and to give a reason.

2. Ask class members to imagine they found out reasons why the person behaves in a negative way and to write the reasons down.

3. Ask class members to share how they feel about the person after realizing there may be a story that explains the negative behavior of the person.

Example: (corresponding to the three points above)

1. I do not want to be friends with Rosie because she never talks to me.

2. I found out that Rosie is unhappy and lonely at home, and she is afraid her Mom may not be able to pay the rent.

3. Now that I know this may be true, I want to be friends with Rosie because her not talking is not about me but about her feelings about what is happening at home.

Post-Exercise Discussion:
1. How has this exercise changed the way you think about people you are afraid of or with whom you do not want to be friends?
2. Imagine how understanding the story of the other person could affect the way people feel and think about their perceived enemies, nations in conflict, and groups of people that you or perhaps others dislike.

Exercise Nine: Imagine Emotions of a Historical Character

Description: This exercise is about understanding the emotions of a historical character. The teacher asks class members to make a list of five people from history and circumstances. Then write emotions that each person may have felt about what was happening in history or in the life of the person when they were experiencing the emotions.

Alternatively, the teacher can make a list of historical people, describe their circumstances, and then invite class members to list emotions the person might have had.

Example: Abraham Lincoln sees slaves being sold in the town square, and in that moment he feels sad that they have no families of their own, angry that men would treat other men as property, and hopeless that he could do nothing about it.

Post-Exercise Discussion:
1. Who would like to share your list of historical people and circumstances with the class?
2. What emotions did you come up with and what are the emotions about?

Exercise Ten: Having Empathy for Anger

Description: This exercise assists the development of ways to cope with the anger of another person by using empathic reflection. Empathy for anger can sometimes have the effect of reducing the anger of a person.

A scenario is demonstrated by the teacher who makes a reflective empathic statement when someone is very angry. After observing this, class members are asked to form pairs and to practice making a reflective empathic statement to the other person who makes an angry statement.

Example: (demonstrated)

Angry Person: "You never do what you're told, and so now I have to do it for you."

Empathic Listener: "You feel angry because I didn't do my work, and that makes more work for you. Is that what you are feeling?"

Following this demonstration, ask class members to enact the same scenario in pairs with each person taking turns being the angry person, then the empathic listener. Use the statements provided in the above example and repeated them to help you feel more of the emotion and what it is like to say and hear the words.

Post-Exercise Discussion:
1. What was it like making the angry statement?
2. What was it like making the empathic reflective statement?
3. What was it like as the angry person hearing the empathic reflective statement of the listener?
4. Imagine how empathic reflection could be used between nations to reduce hostility. How could it work?

About the Author

Daniel Keeran, MSW, has been a counselor and therapist for over 30 years in hospital and private practice settings. He is the author of *Effective Counseling Skills: the practical wording of therapeutic statements and processes*, and the founder and President of the College of Mental Health Counseling giving practical online skill training in counseling, for teachers and other helping professionals.

One Last Favor

On completing the lesson, at our website please provide your brief comments on the outcome and impact on students so that others can be encouraged to use this important lesson.

> Consultation and support at *no charge* is available by email contacting the author at collegemhc@gmail.com